Love's
Smiles & Tears

Love's Smiles and Tears

by
F. C. Appelhanz

Love's Smiles and Tears © 2019 by **F. C. Appelhanz**

Front and back cover artwork, plus artwork for poem "Honey," by **Angela Appelhanz Fitzpatrick**

ISBN-13: 9781794063679

Table of Contents

Sunrise Enchantment

Walking in the succulent dew,
welcoming the sunrise.
My love is in my arms
as nighttime says its good-byes.

Wonderful is the honeysuckle aroma
as nature's minstrels awaken.
My love's eyes smile for me,
and our hearts are thrown open.

The world is serenely beautiful
and apparitions dance in the mist.
This moment is truly magical;
our spirits begin to entwist.

Within this profound experience,
our truth is all we know.
Love whispers ancient mysteries,
as the rhythms of life flow.

Entering the world of daybreak
our souls rejoice and sing;
an eruption of sights and sounds
are the gifts sunrise will bring.

Morning Love

Whisper sweet sounds,
laced with the emotion
of a thousand kisses.
For my body craves
the esoteric ecstasy
of your touch.

Let the world contract
into a singular moment,
as we drift into
a fog of enchantment.
Safely in infinity's embrace,
all questions disappear.

Time is suspended
within two heartbeats,
beating as one.
Two breaths quiver,
melting into each other,
breathing as one.

Love silently simmers,
as arms and legs enfold
the essence of contentment.
Only intimacy can ignite
passion so genuine,
love so real.

Honey

When a sunset reveals its mag-
nificence,
in wondrous hues and delights,
taking my breath away;
I will whisper your name.

In the stillness of a moonlit
night,
enfolding all senses with its se-
renity,
giving my soul reassurance;
I will whisper your name.

As life evolves in heartfelt experi-
ences,
capturing moments of incredible
clarity,
bringing a smile to my heart;
I will whisper your name.

The sound of rain, sight of snow-
flakes,
reminders of intimate conversa-
tions,
causing me to tremble;
I will whisper your name.

Cuddling of lover's fingertips,
while listening with only their
eyes,
witnessing a universe of just two;
I will whisper your name.

Pleasures of consoling assurance,
dwell in your laughter and smile,
when magic stirs the air;
I will whisper your name.

In a baby's eyes, hints of amazing
secrets,
in an embrace of true tenderness,
in a glancing touch of love;
I will whisper…

When the night is completely
silent,
the only sound, one beating
heart,
my soul searching for solace;
I will…

Escape

A plethora of whispers
drift upon midnight air.
I remember conversations;
a voice- soothing and fair.

Bewitching- were her words;
creating a symphony of emotion.
Her eyes slowed time to a trickle;
glowing in natural illumination.

As a full moon rose,
a spontaneous kiss was born.
Spirits of light intertwined,
and night's beauty adorn.

Two lives started to intermingle,
casting away expectations.
Midnight air was electrified;
for love knows no limitations.

My being savors that moment
among the whispers and moon,
when I experienced fulfillment,
and my heart escaped its cocoon.

But Mostly

Love is fickle
unlike a tickle
sometimes just a trickle.
But mostly full-blown.

Love has inclinations
inside mysterious encryption
testing humanity's limitations.
But mostly it just is.

Love is a pinprick
appearing within a limerick
our time continues to tick.
But mostly we just drool.

Love gives us wrinkles
akin to a ripe pickle
contagious as a jingle.
But mostly we live anyway.

While You're Away

Wisps of you linger,
mixed with my yearning
for a heart to heart embrace.

A delicate remembrance of you
is enfolded in the fabric
we shared together.

Still barely audible
is the enchantment of your laughter,
as faint whispers of love
hover in my mind.

A gentle sound to cherish
within my heart alone.

We danced among creativity;
lost in the moment.

The joy within your eyes
enlivened quiet surroundings.

You gave me precious gifts
to comfort me while you're away.

A Beginning

A magnificent moon wears
a mournful hue.
Hopes and dreams wane,
because I love you.

My path has become unfocused;
withered are expectations.
An archaic apparition dances,
toying with my anticipation.

Same mournful moon
cuddles and possesses my heart.
Love knows no logic;
when will serenity start?

Years provided uncertainty,
and my mind a fertile ground.
You came to me in dreams;
stirring emotions profound.

A voice whispering enchantment
awoke a primal yearning.
With unconditional acceptance,
love creates a magical beginning.

To Love You

To love you
is to look
into mystery's eyes
and see infinity's grace.

To love you
is to understand
infinite goodness
connecting with the universe.

To love you
is to whisper
secrets of the mystics.
Completeness within.

To love you
is to feel
a divine presence.
I am whole again.

To love you
is to risk.
Simple and real-
my inspirational gift to us.

Insufficent

Love wasn't enough-
a solitary refrain.
Life continues onward,
singularly again.

Commitment wasn't enough.
Hidden were desires.
Truth was an assassin,
for love's funeral pyre.

Love wasn't enough.
In darkness I cry.
Questions unanswered,
I'll never know why.

Intimacy wasn't enough.
Defects were mine.
Surprising revelations,
revealed by time.

Love wasn't enough.
Nor chocolate or roses.
Retreating inward
my heart slowly closes.

A Whiff of Love

Love pauses a moment,
like a gentle, soothing breeze,
just outside my window.
To enter once again,
upon delicate wings.
Touching my heart, with
familiar whispers of love.
To awaken suppressed memories,
when dramatic feelings were pure.

"Be the authentic me,"
a commitment for my soul.
To absorb the joy,
embrace the pain.
Reawakening my amazing smile,
personality bursting forth.
Love's presence I will embrace,
radiating warmth and excitement.
Lasting a lifetime of reflection.

To love, ignites celebration,
gratitude, memory or longing.
Magical images will dance,
ideas of perfect harmony surface.
Love will flutter around my heart,
causing me to cry cathartic tears,
wonderful expressions of life.
Pausing in a quiet moment,
I will patiently wait in riveted awe.

Beautiful Desire

We stood in the shadow,
of moonlit lace curtains.
Our fingers intertwined
as I kissed her neck,
sensuous and soft.

Our lives issued forth
in words of pure emotion.
Spirits danced with delight,
as our worlds suddenly evolved,
into a maelstrom of passion.

We experienced intimacy's magic,
cocooned in love's authenticity.
Our existence melted together,
as gasp and moans reverberated.
Desires became real.

Illuminated only by moonlight,
we fell into welcoming eyes.
To drift within a timeless moment,
enfolding each other's souls
in an embrace infinite and now.

Enduring Love

Look into my eyes,
See my love growing,
Stronger and deeper.

Every new breath
Gives my life meaning,
Because of your love.

As this journey continues,
Our steps become one,
Seeking each other's touch.

With hearts rejoicing freely,
Memories are created,
Flowing into love unconditional.

Within our tender embrace,
The world bestows a sigh,
Lost in its distractions.

Time is our companion.
Witnessing a love, real,
The world envious and smiling.

In Her Presence

She causes me to smile,
she is beautiful:
in the moonlight,
the candle light,
or morning light.

She touches my heart,
she is remarkable:
in unlimited sharing,
absolute listening,
unconditional loving.

She awakens my spirit,
she is inspiration:
in overwhelming tenderness,
incredible thoughtfulness,
unbelievable uniqueness.

She gives me meaning,
she is integrity:
in her core purity,
her fantastic honesty,
and inspiring intensity.

Romance

To dwell in the midst of your beauty,
I dwell in the midst of my uncertainty.
To wonder, at the depth of your thinking,
I wonder, at my continuing amazement.
To experience your intense tenderness,
I experience unfulfilled longing.
To gaze into your eyes of compassion,
I gaze into the possibilities of life.
To listen to your words of assurance,
I listen to the emotion of my heart.
To accept your unconditional caring,
I accept my limitations to receive.
To cuddle your fingers in everlasting embrace,
I cuddle the meaning and essence of my soul.
To walk the path of your incredible insight,
I walk my path as a master's pupil.
To remember still-frames of moonlit smiles,
I remember my joy at lucid watching.
To dwell in the midst of your beauty,
I dwell in the midst of love.

Irrefutable Love

For lovers enveloped
by a cocoon of contentment.
Time is suspended
as our dreams intermingle.

I kiss your forehead
with tender lips.
You kiss my hand
with love in your eyes.

This moment is ours
to dwell upon forever.
Our lives slowly evolve
with love's soft radiance.

You smile at me
with unrestrained affection.
I will not quell
my heart's extreme joy.

Within our contentment,
our names become meaningless.
Within our embrace,
we celebrate love extraordinaire.

Giving

To my breath,
my meaning,
my constant thought,
Give me your hand.

For a moment,
a life time,
an eternal timelessness,
Dwell deep within me.

Truth declares my emotions,
declares my affirmations,
declares my inspirations,
Embrace the real magic.

I give a tender heart,
I give beautiful joy,
I give genuine love,
Receive the essence of me.

Face of Love

With you beside me,
tenderness becomes my shadow.
A reassuring embrace
will usher in our tomorrow.
Stars smile upon us,
our world tranquil.

With you in my life,
joyful are my tears.
Your captivating eyes,
erase all crippling fears.
Voices speak in silence,
two hearts blend into one.

With you I am whole,
my heart I give completely.
Embracing your amazing love,
creates a soulful harmony.
Whispering our beloved's name,
we will know the face of love.

Relishing it forever.

Beloved

Tell me of your pain,
Tell me of your sorrow.
Guarantees your heart craves,
Guarantees of a better tomorrow.

Let me caress your hand,
Let me touch your soul.
Smother someone with your dreams,
Smother yourself...out of control.

The incredible being you are,
That incredible rock for everyone.
Laughter, that sometimes comes easily,
Laughter, your eyes seep with affection.

See the beauty of your essence,
See all that each moment can be.
Insight, your trusted companion,
Insight, that honesty is the key.

Beautiful is the music of your heart,
Beautiful is the poetry of your smile.
Grateful, that our spirits connected,
Grateful, when our spirits mingled awhile.

Separation

Kiss me once more,
before the toll of the bell.
For with that mournful sound,
sorrowful yearnings will begin.

Already I miss
your caresses and smiles.
I weep; not looking into
your eyes loving and blue.

Time was our companion
in fleeting moments of rapture.
I savor still-frames of you
which enable me to exist.

Within this eternal void,
my heart whispers your name.
My soul wanders aimlessly;
lost is joyful meaning.

I long for another embrace,
and the sunrise will find me;
with an apparition by my side.

Comforting Conformation

To kiss your cheek,
is to embody the essence,
of pure joy.
My heart still yearns,
to be enfolded,
by your love again.

Whispering secret words,
of desire and affection.
As I unconsciously reaffirm,
simple, true devotion,
to the irrefutable
owner of my heart.

Within this interlude,
time patiently waits.
To cuddle esoteric moments
of eternal love.
For in her presence,
I feel comforting confirmation.

Cherish

In the stillness of twilight,
between sorrow and solace,
I hold you in an embrace,
that takes my breath away.
In my dreams,
fantasies become real,
yearnings become fulfilled.
Playful moments linger,
amplifying heart-felt reflection.

Thoughts dance among the memories,
gleeful kisses in bathing moonlight.
Only in quiet slumber
will yearnings rest, to awaken in daydreams.
Daydreams causing my heart
to remember vivid expressions of love.
How your beauty glowed in candlelight,
your smile quickened my heart,
expressive eyes spoke true emotion.

Time cautions life, to not
pause on its journey of discovery.
My soul will cherish forever,
when my heart became yours.

Butterfly, Heart and Light

Heart to heart, mind to mind,
reach into my soul.
Our thoughts will now align,
abandoning vestiges of control.

Arm in arm, hand in hand,
wrap me in your warmth.
With truth, we will understand,
expectations have no worth.

Whisper to whisper, smile to smile,
we dwell among the divine.
Hold me for a great while,
with caresses of a lifetime.

Embrace to embrace, kiss to kiss,
your joy is my delight.
Symbols of our esoteric bliss-
Butterfly, heart and light.

Time within pictures, pictures within time,
continuing our journey-
we partake in simple pleasures
and love permeates us completely.

Love and Forever

The warmth of your body,
trembles in my hands,
accentuating a fool's folly,
to resist my heart's command.

Pure passion begins to surface,
captured by oil lamp illumination,
souls intertwine in spiritual embrace,
dancing in love's celebration.

Moments in soft, flickering light,
caresses release raw emotions,
inhibitions set free to take flight,
mystifying joy knows no limitations.

Looking into your eyes,
tenderness and compassion, I see,
believing there are no good-byes,
the poetry of you overwhelms me.

Memories of comforting affection,
bewitching experiences esoteric,
a present for my mind's contemplation,
draped in moonlight's unique magic.

Closeness time will not dissolve,
encounter of unbridled, pure pleasure,
as our lives continue to evolve,
your remarkable gift I will treasure forever.

(Part 1, Trilogy of Love)

Love and Fantasy

Time has no meaning or power,
when you look into my eyes.
A sense of comforting acceptance,
overwhelms fear, reassuring my sighs.
Adventurous mystery flashes in your smile,
hints of the excitement you epitomize.
Touch of a finger, stroke of an arm,
messages from a spirit confident and wise.

Passion knows no boundaries,
tenderly holding you in an embrace.
Whispered words of divine joy,
enchanting moments time cannot displace.
Together we exist in spiritual harmony,
interweaving with amazing grace.
Memories of your healing thoughtfulness,
overshadow trivial, trite disgrace.

Affection is pure, meaningful and sincere,
giving unconditionally my heart.
Discovering love's paradise with a kiss,
intense yearning awakens when we part.
Laughter, remarkable in its soulfulness,
enthralled by bedazzling art.
Specters of inner doubts finally dissipate,
replaced by love's magic, swelling in my heart.

(Part 2, Trilogy of Love)

Love's Smiles and Tears

Love and Friendship

Unexplained love,
surrounds my heart.
A swelling of emotions,
induces tears of tenderness.
Music pacifies my soul,
intimacy resides within caressing.
Pictures of your smile,
occupy my mind endlessly.
A glancing touch of romance,
explodes into rampant passion.

Excitement issues from fingertips,
hearts sing pure rapture.
Spirits exposed and vulnerable,
give a priceless gift of love.
Words of truthful affection,
touch the essence of our core.
Whispers of inner voices,
resonate within simple laughter,
dancing around the question,
will true, real love,
my heart capture.

(Part 3, Trilogy of Love)

Love Experienced

I miss you,
in the way you kissed
my shoulder before sleeping.
I dreamed of you.

In the way you smiled,
knowing my difficulty
with loving you so much.
I muddled through.

In the way you sighed
at life's inequalities.
Insanity expressed by others.
I saw raw frustration.

In the way your wayward spirit
gave a lifelong memory
of roses in moonlight.
I stay amazed.

In the way you cried
for all small creatures,
enfolded in your heart.
I witnessed the true you.

In the way you helped
me to continue onward,
sorrowful, yet enriched.
I experienced love.

Esoteric Encounter

Eyes speak silent laughter,
trusting in spiritual conviction.
Knowledge of a loving truth,
providing guidance and inspiration.
Teaching with words of sincerity,
weaving a caring connection.

Smile, and a tender heart emerges,
reaching out with invisible fingers.
Love caresses raw wounds of insecurity,
to enfold life in soothing whispers.
As affection flows effortlessly,
the joy of real acceptance lingers.

Occasions of spontaneous fidelity,
voicing heartfelt, core insights.
Expounding enchanting openness,
goodness enshrouded by light.
Witnessing hopeful sharing,
reassures everything will be all right.

With quiet, timeless memories,
cherished pictures remain constant.
Thoughts of a charming spirit remain,
simple reflections of a soul so vibrant.
Distance has no barriers or restrictions,
upon intimacy, magnificent and radiant.

Another

Another day,
discovering you.
A daily declaration,
"I love you."

Another moment,
looking into your eyes.
An esoteric moment,
together at sunrise.

Another embrace,
rapture is mine.
Embracing my beloved
sensations for a lifetime.

Another gift,
true miracle, within mystery.
Love's unconditional gift,
source of wonderment to me.

Triggers

Within my mind,
I hear your voice.
Triggering a pang
of a loving refrain.

Glimpsing a photo,
I see your smile.
Triggering a heaviness,
that constantly lingers.

Discovering an artifact,
I remember a moment.
Triggering pent-up tears,
that never erase anguish.

In everyday moments,
my thoughts are of you.
Triggering a question,
of unconditional love.

Whispers in my dreams,
reveal my heart's uncertainty.
Triggering a fearful realization,
I may never love again.

Intimacy

In this serene, quiet moment,
we cuddle each other, and
whisper "I love you."

We are oblivious
to all distractions,
breathing in harmony,
and lost in dreams of passion.

As we embrace
draped in each other's arms,
time is suspended,
in the rapture of tranquility.

Murmurs speak volumes,
caresses erupt in emotion,
hearts beat as one.
There is only US.

This moment is truly ours.
A moment within
eternity's embrace.

May we never let go.

Forever Entwined

When the highest of mountains
are whittled to mere clumps,
of small homes for tiny creatures,
Our love will remain.

When the oceans of the world,
dwindle to small puddles,
oases for tiny blades of grass,
Our love will remain.

When the sound of many voices
shrinks to a single syllable,
to wither and disappear,
Our love will remain.

For our love knows no limits
of earthly time or space.
Amongst the enlightened spirits,
Our love will remain.

Imprinted by hope
enveloped by goodness,
Our spirits forever will be entwined.

Love's Smile

Out of the wasteland,
I will venture forth.
Wasteland of broken hearts,
I will dwell within you no more.

I will take no more caution,
I'll build no more walls,
I'll not pause in hesitation,
Love's entrancing voice calls.

Lost within an emotional haze,
true feelings drift neglected.
An inimical, yet kind haze-wanes,
Love's calling now accepted.

I'm accepting the pitfalls,
I understand the vulnerability,
I'll accept all the rapture,
Life has exposed its ecstasy.

Truth, in all its enchantment,
truth in all its wonder,
truth in all its bewilderment,
resounding in my heart once again.

A Heart Worth Saving

Take this heart,
possessing many layers.
Consequences of life's experiences,
tragic memories reverberate,
among loved ones silently abandoned.
Gripping, numbing pain,
creates doubting, wishful assurance.
A layer applied to continue,
a layer grows to cope.

Take this heart,
wounded, yet beating.
Sadness and guilt enshroud this heart.
Forced to accept past mistakes,
entombed in a world of no choices.
Craving to feel alive again,
it cries for genuine affection.
A layer to protect,
a layer that somehow dreams.

Take this heart,
sheltered in comforting solitude.
A core pure and tender,
slowly fades into itself,
feeling no emotions of affection.
Celebrating love, doubtful,
unable to radiate joy.
A layer to recall hurts,
A layer covering goodness.

Take this heart,
caress its callousness.
Create strength with gentle words.
Coax real sensitivity.
Removing a lifetime of layers.
Whisper beautiful phrases,
freedom to feel expressive again.
Cuddled in a loving embrace.
A heart worth saving.

A Loving Encounter

Let go, give love a try,
as stars dance in a cloudless sky.
Let's spend precious time together,
the world will intrude sometime later.
Tell me your most cherished dreams,
hand in hand among moon beams.
Time suspends its journey awhile,
when love expresses a tender smile.
In stunning green eyes, your goodness grows,
beauty witnessed within a perfect rose.
Magical embraces among the fireflies,
whispering my affection, a soft reprise.
Enchanting, terse moments we spend,
fleeting, as a candle's flame in the wind.
Believing our trusting hearts will tell,
secrets where only truth can dwell.
Giving of each other in language of old,
vulnerability that's beautiful to behold.
Swaying and laughing with the caressing breeze,
in hypnotic movement among the trees.
Souls intertwine in spiritual ecstasy,
soaring to heights in childlike simplicity.

A Tender Heart

Give compassionate care
to my battered heart.
Born of fear and caution
as it survives still.

Through emotional mazes
I created senselessly,
love withstood all doubt,
lurking in suspicion.

Guided by simple trust,
vulnerability awakes.
Bonds of common desire
provide a soulful connection.

Oh, the joyful emotions
an open heart evokes.
Giving the world its goodness
and quiet inspiration.

Trusting, I affirm
my heart has shed its chains.
True love I give to you,
without restrictions.

Us

Within our world,
our hearts beat in unison.
Guided by esoteric memories,
born a thousand years ago.

Journeying in search of
the smile we both recognize.
For spirits intuitively know,
true love in a touch.

Time, kept us apart;
time brought us together.
Rapture is our embrace,
eternity is our separation.

Frozen is the moment
when our lips found their home.
Emotion was electrifying
as our bodies reconnected.

Our hearts belong to each other,
our fondness knows no limits,
laughter, the music we dance to,
love, playing the melody.

Kisses

A kiss
in the morning
before the sun
sheds its night's garment.
Sensual and beautiful.

A kiss
in a corner
at a public place
causes embarrassment.
Spontaneous silliness.

A kiss
for a toll,
anywhere or anytime,
a poignant, loving moment.
Laughter so genuine.

A kiss
in the moonlight,
tender and sweet,
for our enjoyment.
Cuddling each other's spirit.

A kiss
as we pass each other
letting lips reveal
affection's poetic statement.
Embracing the future.

A kiss
in loving arms,
succulent and real,
an intimate wonderment.
The world is ours.

A Lingering Desire

Waiting, waiting, waiting for
an embrace given wholeheartedly.
My existence seems to implore
the smile that fulfills me.
A gentle, fun spirit I adore
awakens a childhood memory.
With integrity at her core,
laughter erupts spontaneously.
An aura of love I gladly wore,
expressions of affection for all to see.
For her kiss I will wait forevermore
because they are given with sincerity.
Life is ours to experience and savor.
She gives life authenticity.
Opportunities to open love's door,
awoke as I gave my heart willingly.
Love's elixir I will constantly explore,
enhancing my simple life completely.
Intoxicating emotions I cannot ignore
as I await her presence longingly.
While daydreaming of kisses galore,
patiently waiting, I will be.

Lament

Look away, your pain I see,
emotions of anguish engulf me.
Raw feelings we cannot ignore,
when simple, guarded truth,
tore our lives apart.

Forgiveness seems a hollow request,
to ease a hurt that may never rest.
With memories of an emotional toll,
sadness has enveloped my soul,
struggling to survive.

Greetings and laughter no longer radiate,
displaced by flashes of distrust or hate.
The still frame of a last embrace,
tears of woeful heartbreak do not erase,
guilt that haunts continuously.

The presence of doubtful assurance,
brings fear of mistaken confidence.
Weight of heartfelt blame limitless,
coping with frequent regrets endless.
Will a heart ever heal?

Into Us

With whispers of tenderness,
you take my hand.
Together, we disappear
into imagination's wonderland.

Incredible moments of rapture
suspend our lives in time.
Hearts seep into each other
given the freedom to intertwine.

Intimacy simple and profound
envelopes naked, human spirits.
Dormant, true emotions rejoice,
overwhelming all petty regrets.

Beautiful messages are shared
in words ancient and mystical.
With bare souls, we smile.
Our serenity is magical.

As echoes of pure softness
fill our every pore,
the gentlest of touches spread,
caressing each other's exposed core.

Within a glow of mutual love,
our universe enjoys tranquility.
Within our enchanting embrace
lies a world of amazing mystery.

Intimate

Call to me:
let me hear your voice singing,
melodies of pure inspiration,
move my soul once more.

Look to me:
let me see your smiling face,
awaken dormant admiration, at
your beautiful goodness.

Reach to me:
let me feel love by touching.
A callous heart rekindles slowly,
nurtured by your compassion.

Sigh to me:
let me comfort your longing,
words of tenderness and wonder,
guiding your spirit onward.

Whisper to me:
let me share in your dreaming,
realm of endless experiences,
adventures born with imagination.

Come to me:
let me dwell in your giving,
my being receiving your gifts,
unconditional joy and love.

Loving Arms

My loving arms
will hold you
as the moon and stars
witness your smile.

When the world
encroaches into
your moments of serenity,
these arms
will caress
the pain away.

Because real love
knows only
authenticity,
these arms
will enfold you
in a meaningful embrace.

With arms outstretched,
my heart connects with you;
absorbing
your essence
and amazed
by your uniqueness.

My loving arms
believe
in no boundaries.
Your
loving heart
makes
my spirit soar.

All Of You

In the stillness of contentment,
calming is final acceptance,
I will love all of you.

In the rapture of the moment,
joy has overshadowed reluctance.
Your breath becomes my breath.

In shimmering moments of excitement,
affection dances in luminous brilliance.
Your heart becomes my heart.

In an eclipse of pure wonderment
draped within a magical fragrance,
Your dream becomes my dream.

In voiceless words of enchantment,
our souls quiver, lost in romance.
Your touch becomes my touch.

In our shared entanglement,
we accept our defects within balance.
Your imperfection becomes my imperfection.

In our emotional lucidity resides amazement.
Simple phrases gain their importance.
Your giving becomes my giving.

Falling in Love

The night breeze sings,
phrases of tenderness and comfort.
Moonlight's magic brings,
enchanting whispers into the night.
Moments of heartfelt enjoyment,
amplify truth in unbridled emotion.

Witness beautiful spirits dancing,
spellbound to the unique gift of themselves.
Playful figures pause, in joyful listening,
while our world sways in rhythmic ecstasy.
Wonderful feelings, erupt spontaneously,
as we give our hearts to love.

Gift

When hearing your voice,
I listen, mesmerized,
to the song in my heart.
You're beautiful in candlelight;
a flickering flame of hope;
as wonderous sensations start.
Gliding, tender fingers
engulf my awareness,
spontaneous expression of art.

Gazing into your eyes
I suddenly experience,
joyful, real affection.
Doubts of my earthly purpose
dissolve in your embrace,
reaffirming soulful admiration.
Perfection in a simple kiss,
moves my soul to tremble;
happiness knows no limitation.

Images of your smile
remain radiant;
reassurance for doubtful moments.
Awaken my dormant worthiness,
cultivate unbridled intimacy;
spirits remaining benevolent.
Your gifts of personal compassion,
gifts manifested through action.
The gift of your wonderful life.

Love and Devotion

With each flicker of flame,
my heart whispers your name.
Eternity to short a time,
holding you in my mind.
Each day my soul awakens,
realizing love not forsaken.
Gazing into incredible eyes,
our hearts know no lies.
Love's intensity causes me to tremble,
spirits soar to heights unbelievable.
With the thought of your affection,
boundless soar moments of adoration.
When fingers caress and intertwine,
we experience connections sublime.
Enchanting music fills our space,
accompanying a magical embrace.
Feelings of joyful acceptance,
allow no barriers to destroy us.
In your presence I feel completeness,
solidified by unconditional kindness.
Time encourages respect to grow,
amplifying what lovers know.

The magic of pure love and devotion.

Moonlight Magic

Words to say
time to play.
Heart ablaze,
mind in a daze.

Life feels good,
as it should.
See you soon,
under the moon.

Look into my eyes,
witness, there, no lies.
Whisper secret desires,
ignite passionate fires.

Kiss me tenderly,
expressed sincerely.
Release all inhibition,
feel a soulful connection.

Into you I see,
love's excitement set free.
Our emotions will soar,
all fears will be no more

Caressing each other,
reassuring one another.
Let hearts intertwine,
our faults remain blind

Heartfelt feelings so true,
my love given to you.

Mischievous Mystery

You come to me in dreams,
I love you in moonlight.
Take my hand,
lead me to innermost secrets.
Our souls know no boundaries,
united in an embrace into nothingness.
In timeless wonder of each other,
acceptance of imperfections eternal.
You sense my desires,
I marvel at your uniqueness.

We dwell in the moment,
cuddled by simplistic heartbeats.
Caresses in silent admiration, to
the power of unconditional sharing.
Spirits dance, soar and intertwine,
in exhaustive flashes of ecstasy.
Melodies of the heart,
flow in unbridled smiles of truth.
Eagerly, wishes will reveal,
hidden, unspoken rapture.

Gifts of wonderous tenderness,
shared in the magic of affection.
We savor love's celebration,
discovering keys to limitless comfort.
Worlds revolve around us,
blind to the power of real emotion.
Laughter pouring from your heart,
warms me with its sincerity.
The beautiful light of your memory,
beacon for wonderment and joy.

Regrets

A smile that slowly faded,
A sigh that grew in intensity,
A hope that in time felt jaded,
A love that struggles with sincerity.

As memories of caressing fingers lessen,
As ardent passion enfolds, then withers,
As moments of emotion yearn to be awaken,
As tears cascade from a hurt that angers.

And a heartfelt embrace will be missed,
And romance will not dance in the eyes,
And a soul cries when no longer kissed,
And words of tender affection twist into lies.

Amid sorrow that stifles the beauty of living,
Amid uncertainty that seeps into every thought,
Amid doubts resolution will bring insightful meaning.
Amid a loss that lessons of intimacy taught.

Apart

As hours drift,
in ever widening circles,
memories will suffice,
'til we meet again.

Moments of trauma
surface in intermittent waves.
A distant, familiar voice
soothes my active mind.

Naked emotions wither,
succumbing to onslaughts of doubt.
Affection extends its hands,
a lifeline for my sanity.

As grace slumbers,
within its forest of everything—
I will draw guidance
from silent, decaying leaves.

Your voice whispers,
amidst wild, untamed currents.
Torrents of inner solace sing
songs of reassurance.

Loving

Vivid memories surface,
ambivalence, gives a wink.
Love's draconian insanity,
pushes reality to the brink.

Waves of distorted reasoning,
become unacceptable clutter.
As heartfelt recollections,
tug at a true believer.

With the gift of love,
all rationality is lost.
Real love is immeasurable,
blind to hidden cost.

As I sadly, endlessly adjust,
within moments of anguish.
By embracing fond experiences,
love's ecstasy is mine to relish.

Still

Whispers of seconds gone by,
cling to moments in my memory.
Carrying me into reflection, upon
love's constant yearning.

I'm befuddled by the wistfulness
I experienced—thinking of you.
Dancing inside my imagination
are snippets of enchantment.

Esoteric stills of emotions-
framed in a subjective reality
are expressed in isolation.
Moments thinking to myself
champion an uncertain resolve.

Momentary, minute, triggers of affection
perpetuate my grasping for answers.
Elements of life's living
challenge a questioning mind.
Choices stay concealed in fondness,
and I am reluctant to accept "forever."

You're in my thoughts.
You're in my dreams.
You cradle my heart.

Still.

The Loving Tree

The wind whispers
over the meadows,
hand-in-hand
with moonlight's touch.
My love awaits me
under the loving tree.

My restless footsteps quicken.
They float over obstacles,
both imaginary and real.
Quickening with desire,
rustling the air,
and racing with time.
For my love awaits me
under the loving tree.

I yearn for a glimmer
of a beauty which radiates forever.
A calling of emotions
beckons within, embracing
into nothingness, as
my searching fingers tremble.
My love awaits
under the loving tree.

Invisible spirits dance.
Twirling light absorbs truth.
Hearts intertwine naked.
Timeless love smiles again
under the loving tree.

For the Sake of Loving

Within my heart resides
a feeling—subconscious.
A subtle, profound emotion;
overwhelmingly joyous.

Beautiful words of affection
won't wither before lust.
The desires of the body
succumb to fidelity and trust.

As this journey continues,
producing moments of rapture,
smiles and frowns will intertwine,
and our hearts choose nurture.

Your pain is my pain;
Your ecstasy, my ecstasy;
Your sorrow, my sorrow;
Your love, my love.

Loving for the sake of loving.

Sincere Love

I've looked into your eyes,
all of these sixty years.
Seen your smiles and frowns,
and shared your deepest fears.

Through all of our hardships,
one emotion remained clear.
My love for you never faltered,
your love remained sincere.

Our journey was fraught with trials,
and solutions would always appear.
Life gave us many challenges;
laughter was mixed with tears.

As time destroyed our bodies,
my arms would hold you near.
In our darkest hours,
you would call me, "dear."

Our love has withstood time,
twilight whispers in our ears.

Woe

You destroyed my smile,
such a sad, sad day.
Words seem inept,
words cannot say.
How deep the pain!
How deep the wound!
Only time will alter,
a course littered with emotions.

You silenced my heart,
such a huge, huge loss.
No meaningful guidance,
my soul wanders, lost.
Where will I find solace?
Where will I find strength?
Only serenity can save,
a being devoid of light.

You crushed the joy of living,
such a raw, raw agony.
Thoughts of you linger,
thoughts confuse endlessly.
Wishing you could have expressed,
wishing you could have opened.
Living with a constant truth.
My love for you was real.

Whispered Word

As I enfold you
in loving arms,
thoughts pirouette and sway,
as tender whispers resonate.

Whispered words of affection
escape my feeble mind,
for we are all that exist,
whispering our intimacy.

Expressing complete devotion
in words spoken sincerely,
composed of ardent love,
soft whispers are absorbed.

The faintest of sound
causes us to quake,
in a spell of contentment,
our whispers permeate.

Whispered words create
a cocoon of contentment,
for within our quiet speech,
dwells timeless love.

Suspended in a moment,
our whispers caress us
with profound words
only we will know.

Night Time Yearnings

There is a neglected spot;
where my love sometimes resides.
A spacious void representing
the yearning in my heart.

My hand unconsciously reaches
for the most tender of touches.
My trembling fingers grasp
only a remnant of your presence.

I remember soft laughter
while you dreamed.
Gaiety echoed throughout the room,
then faded away into memories.

As I wallow in my desire,
for a physical confirmation,
Love's voice gently whispers,
"She will soon return."

Within those reassuring words,
my soul enjoys some solace.
I will draw upon thoughts
of kisses in the moonlight
or silly, spontaneous moments.
Cuddling, so simple and warm,
and a love true and real.

"I will be with you in dreams."

Touching My Essence

Touch me, that I may experience
the intensity of your affection.
My body, against yours,
our spirits, absorbing each other,
my heart, open and accepting.

Touch me, that I may marvel
at the sincerity in your eyes.
Emotions, explored together,
my core exposed to you,
as our lives intertwined.

Touch me, so we are one
then we will know rapture.
Truth explodes with honesty.
Grace me by your presence,
let your smile ensnare my heart.

Touch me, then I'll know
strength in unconditional love.
Your words unravel chaos,
laughter, I have never known.
Your reassuring silence soothes my doubt.

Touch me, so I may quietly rest
in the cuddling of your arms.
Tender fingers stroking my face,
cradling my pain with understanding,
fondling my weariness softly.

Touch me, make me realize
the gift of your incredible passion.
Open arms, inviting intimacy,
caress me with dedication and
mystify me with your every breath.

Thoughts From Afar

Listening to resounding quiet,
flowing in ancient waves,
out of the darkness.

In this moment of solitude,
my world revolves around you,
a kindred spirit,
spiritual and alive.

Within your maelstrom,
lie secrets subliminal.
Without your smile,
I gaze upon
a wasteland of thoughts.

I scribble upon this paper,
trying to capture the euphoria
of holding you in my arms.
Beyond waves of tranquility,
dwell my sanctuaries of salvation.

For within the darkness,
lie the seeds of love.
My torment becomes transparent
when your voice I hear.

The Essence of Her

See you in my mind,
touch you in my dreams,
feel you in my heart,
knowing love's wonderful extremes.

Time delays its journey,
a spectator to your sleeping,
mesmerized by the loveliness,
your unpretentious breathing.

Ensnared by your smile,
your keen, green eyes,
intense your sizzling anger,
when encountering deceitful lies.

The universe a passing beholder,
marveling at such integrity,
witnessing unbridled tenderness,
moments of pure simplicity.

Pleasure in unconditional emotion,
inflamed by a lingering glance,
a warm swelling around my heart,
the rapture of your romance.

Touching

Hold my hands
for a limitless duration.
Make my yearnings tolerable
to withstand our separation.

My spirit craves
your gentile, finger connection.
Your eyes reflect quiet,
esoteric inspiration.

Within a mystical aura,
we generate wordless conversation.
You, with an enchanting smile;
I, lost in befuddled admiration.

Time holds its breath
mesmerized by love's illumination.
The world's thunderous sounds
muffled by soulful affection.

Hold my hands,
in beautiful, true contemplation.
As hours slip into radiance,
our lives become a blissful continuation.

Struggling

Tell my heart
answers to painful questions.
Give me true words,
so, smiles appear again.
Remove raw shadows,
make all doubts trivial.
Love should be joyous,
why so complex?
Emotions soar and plummet,
inner tranquility a shamble.
Tears, a temporary relief,
cleansing old, deep scares.
Sadness envelopes a cure,
devoid of reassuring hope.

Tell my heart,
secrets cannot destroy truth.
Show a simple path,
so, respect can shine pure light.
Remove the evil fingers,
gripping with constant fear.
Feelings seem distorted,
everything unfocused.
I crave closeness,
but receive encrypted vagueness.
Whisper something soothing,
make longing swell with ecstasy.
Don't let my heart wither.
A wonderful jewel struggling.

Smile for Me

Give me one moment;
cause the stars to sing.
A present of pure excitement,
giving my heart new wings.
Emotions suddenly awaken,
a result of tender caring.
Smile for me.

Confer me a treasure;
fill the air with electricity.
Show me life's meaning,
stark in its simplicity.
Whisper words of contentment,
enchant my vision with beauty.
Smile for me.

Offer me memories;
laughter, as well as tears.
Strength for times of weakness,
courage overcoming fears.
Touch my soul with your goodness,
special gifts through the years.
Smile for me.

Wishes

I wish for you,
roses, surprising you
in loving offerings.
Many times, whispering,
fragrances and colors
of affection.

I wish for you,
kisses, touching you
in magical embraces.
Heartfelt, real emotion,
remembrances and feelings
of passion.

I wish for you,
smiles, moving you
in radiant expressions.
Amazing, simple beauty,
laughter and pleasure
of no limitation.

I wish for you,
adventures, comforting you
with wonderful memories.
Flashes of excitement,
challenges and rewards
of discovery.

I wish for you,
A lifetime of fulfillment,
A lifetime of love.

Waiting

Pausing a moment,
my heart reaffirms,
feelings my mind resist.
Whispers of love stir
calm, guarded hesitation,
heartfelt happiness persists.
This stirring of emotion,
dormant for so long,
slowly ushers in joyful bliss.

Love reignites memories,
of laughter and elation.
The world discovered anew.
Solitary, doubtful waiting
created paralyzing walls.
I slowly, steadily withdrew.
A commitment for my soul,
challenges the darkness,
my integrity remaining true.

Through senseless waiting,
I have finally become
who I was meant to be.
Love my patient guide
on life's tricky pathway,
with nudges of sincerity.
Marveling at the possibilities,
born from an open heart...
a heart of authenticity.

Embrace the Adventure

Yonder

Yonder my beloved cries,
as her past constantly tries,
to dominate and prevent,
a joyful, free present.

False, shadowy comfort belies,
memories that only stigmatize,
controlling her existence,
by destroying futile resistance.

In a cocoon of isolation,
she endures haunting apparitions,
taunting her with the past,
for hopeful wishes never last.

Yonder my beloved contemplates,
gatherings where love radiates,
in heartfelt, fleeting embraces,
I experience love's true graces.

A Time For Love

In this lifetime,
does love come often?
In the gentlest of heart whispers,
warmth in sincere affection.

Can love's simple pleasure
be complicated by barriers?
Rendered fleeting by neglect,
subdued by circumstances.

Will true love be unconditional?
Given time to express itself.
Enfolding a doubtful heart,
encouraging memories of forever.

Is life worth living
without love as a companion?
Love giving it meaning,
exploding in unbridled freedom.

Choices we make, choices we live,
experiences we love, experiences
we accept.
Intuitive opportunities, intuitive
murmurs, for
A time for love

Take IT!

Take this heart;
no longer viable.
Resuscitate with fingers;
tender, loving and reliable.

Countless, past moments
render it unsalvageable.
Heartache and fear
expose questions unanswerable.

Take this sadness
dwelling deep within.
Give it shape
so hope can begin.

It never believed
loving to be a sin.
It continues to grieve;
will this heart flourish again?

Take it and restore,
all abilities and joy.

Take it into your own;
I believe in you.

Inward Observation

Listen to my heart
broken, yet still beating.
Rejection a symptom,
love was the culprit.
My heart struggles mightily,
as there seems no cure.

Poignant are small memories,
esoteric closeness so real.
A love undeniable
simmers against doubt.
Constant is a yearning
for healing through acceptance.

Emotions will heed
to eventual finality.
A reluctant happiness
is bestowed to another.
Listening to my heart;
it whispers, "courage."

Love's Wondrous Gift

Elusive to some,
intimate to others.
Within delightful smiles
of wonderment
or coy, playful emotions
of bewilderment.
You may sense love's wizardry,
remembering unrestrained happiness.

A transformed heart
will sing love's joy.
Resounding in explosive,
constant certainty, creating
perplexing, frightening sensations,
both wishful and enthralling.
Love zings your heart
with a warm, joyous glow.

Falling in love,
what a magical spell.
To fall in love,
what a wondrous gift.

My Joy

What a joy it is
to tell her I love her.
My heart palpitates,
as emotion rings true and real.

The wonder of her brings
tears of unsuspecting glee.
Thoughts of her, my sole companion
when her embrace I cannot feel.

Inexpressible memories are created-
as we walk in the dew.
Within the beauty of everything
our secrets we reveal.

My love and inspiration,
she whispers her affection.
As two intrepid spirits soar-
journeying at will.

What infinity would be;
her smiles would be too few.
Mystery in her eyes- mischievous;
and as beautiful as the songbird's trill.

Watching

To watch you sleeping,
I dream,
with my eyes open.
Caught in a moment, of
enchantment and beauty.
The soft song of candlelight
floats in the air-
symphonic interweaving of
Magic and Love.
A beautiful vision of slumber,
suspended in quiet refuge,
embraces a momentary solace.
To watch you sleeping,
I surrender,
my heart to you.

Smoldering Love

As my time ebbs,
in ever frequent moments.
I remember a love,
continuously smoldering.
Igniting a small flame,
thawing frozen reluctance.
Love patiently waits.
Faintly recalling romance.
Joy knew no restrictions,
emotions were real, passionate.

As my memory awakens,
embracing unfavorable feelings.
I remember a fondness
buried beneath suspicion.
Love arrives unexpectantly,
constantly in my thoughts.
A yearning blankets my heart
with wishful, trepid hope.
Reality plays its part,
gutting dreams with realism.

I recall her smile,
radiant and welcoming.

Time, Love

Time will judge,
my love for you.
In quiet possibilities,
in assured grandeur.
Never wavering,
a constant companion.

Time cannot diminish,
something so strong.
Emanating authenticity,
in a feeling so real.
True emotion celebrating,
a lifelong journey.

Time will hopefully clarify,
"love knows no logic."
In the joy of its rapture,
amid unquestioned validity.
A heart's barriers shattered,
as conflicts go ever onward.

Time goes painfully slow,
within a haze of quiet grief.
My heart cries for you,
in waves of sad wistfulness.
My heart will remain luminous.
My love will withstand time.

F.C. Appelhanz

Bewildering

My beloved dwells yonder
between reality and deception.
Longingly, her being yearns
for believable truth.
Her remembrances of yesterday's
snippets of love;
apparitions from past years,
barricade an altruistic heart.

Frequently, she visits my dreams
in disguises beautiful and small.
Within an emotional vortex I dare
set free my love's imagination.
Beholding her smile at the door
constantly haunts my existence.
Bewildering is this devotion
to a union unattainable.

Beyond- my heart resides
as an outcast remnant.
Moments of remarkable, real love
are lasting in their effect.
Times we shared will be remembered
within still-frames of affection.
Now, I must fearlessly rediscover
the magic of love's embrace.

Three Kisses

Three kisses in the morning,
and I am on my way.
Off to the factory
to earn my pay.
Though two loving arms,
beckon me to stay.
I've got to earn a living.
I know no other way.

Remembrance of those kisses
makes all obstacles okay.
Our unwavering affection
creates an intimate play.
An embrace waits for me
at the end of each day.
Two intertwined hearts
strut, twirl and sway.

With three kisses in the morning,
all problems fade away.
Smooches give my day meaning,
launching a hushed hooray.
When life tries to interfere,
bringing those clouds of gray,
I just think of the morning;
love is the best influence anyway.

Deliverance

These thirteen years
I have sheltered my love,
in a silent room,
hidden and locked away.
Meandering through life,
ignoring assigned feelings,
hoping to share love, someday.

Within this hiatus
I have worn my armor.
Attachment now complete,
to hide the beautiful, me.
Living a creed of no weakness,
showing no vulnerability,
or tenderness-something few will see.

Because of doubt
my love has hibernated.
A soothing whisper at midnight,
comfort for my silent tears.
Unwilling to abandon my dreams,
unwavering are memories,
powerful moments when darkness clears.

Enduring this interruption
my soul has slumbered.
Time will open my eyes,
as I become who I was meant to be.
Uplifting, the discovery,
rewarding new found tranquility.
Overdue, I will set my wonderful heart free.

When

When I remember
softly embracing you,
I reflect upon
kisses, both electrifying and haunting.
Pure emotion courses through me.
The caressing of your eyes
told me your truth.

When I enfolded
your beautiful apparition
in my dreams of yesterday,
my being became smitten
to depths I could not fathom.
Only in my loss,
love became an enigma.

When I struggle
to accept your rejection,
my ambivalence lingers
in memories of you.
My heart was enflamed.
We were in love
when your words surrounded my essence.

F.C. Appelhanz

Reflections

In between moments,
of rapture or despair.
I remember your,
eyes of excitement
and air of adventure.

When stillness abounds,
my poetry electrified.
I feel your spirit,
touching my exposed core,
intertwining our lives.

Intermittent, lucid memories,
overwhelm my existence.
I struggle to accept:
our intimacy's finality,
whispered words silenced,
absent, heartfelt embraces,
love's voice, a lingering apparition.

Expectations

Will you read for me
when my eyes become cloudy
from constantly looking within?
With words of melodic magic,
will you caress
my expectations to sleep?

Will I believe in you
without the odorless stench
from expectant cravings?
My insecurities are
persistent, living between
our creative worlds.

Will you share tenderness
as my expectations become
callous from many years of denial?
As I stretch the boundaries
of ecstasy in ways unimaginable.
Will you understand?

Will I unconditionally
accept leaving my heart
open to the uncertainty of time?
Drawing upon Love's assurance,
one cannot avoid Truth.

Expectations only destroy.

Love

If you appear to me,
I may not recognize you.
Time has not been kind
as I experienced the true you.
Snippets of old emotions
fail to completely feel you.
Misinterpreting signals
brings out the enigma of you.
Whispers surround my heart
whenever I am near you.
Questions of my worthiness
haunt the memory of you.
As my life hastens forward,
I reflect more upon you.
Dreams of formless beauty
expose the wonder of you.
Within an enchanting voice
rapture is expressed by you.
Because you are Love
unconditionally you will find me.

Heart Warming Wishes

To embrace you
is to envelope the essence of my heart.

To kiss you
is to visit ecstasy's presence.

To hear you
is to experience yearning for laughter.

To walk with you
is to journey down the path of romance.

To see you
is to dream within enchantments realm.

To miss you
is to feel love's true meaning.

To remember you
is to smile at a joyous, heartfelt union.

Listing by First Lines:

Acknowledgements

I want to take this opportunity to thank **Carol Yoho** for her excellent technical support and help with this project. Her suggestions and observations were greatly appreciated.

Also, I want to thank **Angela Appelhanz Fitzpatrick** for the beautiful artwork for the front and back covers and the insert for the poem "Honey."

About the Poet: Fred C. Appelhanz

As with many of his fellow humans, the author has experienced the manic euphoria and the enigmatic loss of "being in love". The difference being, he expresses it in poetic form. There becomes a time in our lives when we have experienced the many opportunities of loving and being loved. The author continues to look forward to the next time love expresses itself to him, in all its allure.

Made in the USA
Middletown, DE
07 August 2022

70454315R00057